FINDING WAKÂ

JAYSEN'S STORY

© 2020 by Eschia Books Inc.

Printed in Canada

All rights reserved. No part of this work covered by the copyrights hereon may be reproduced or used in any form or by any means—graphic, electronic or mechanical—or stored in a retrieval system or transmitted in any form by any means without the prior written permission of the publisher, except for reviewers, who may quote brief passages. Any request for photocopying, recording, taping or storage on information retrieval systems of any part of this work shall be directed in writing to the publisher.

The Publisher: Eschia Books Inc.

Library and Archives Canada Cataloguing in Publication
Title: Jaysen's story / by Jaysen Flett-Paul ; illustrated by Chloe "Bluebird" Mustooch.
Names: Flett-Paul, Jaysen, author.
Description: Series statement: Finding Wakâ
Identifiers: Canadiana (print) 20190199520 | Canadiana (ebook) 20190199628 | ISBN 9781926696829 (softcover) | ISBN 9781926696836 (EPUB)
Subjects: LCSH: Flett-Paul, Jaysen. | LCSH: Flett-Paul, Jaysen—Mental health. | LCSH: Indigenous peoples—Suicidal behavior—Canada—Prevention. | CSH: Native peoples—Suicidal behavior—Canada—Prevention. | CSH: Native peoples—Canada—Rites and ceremonies. | CSH: Native peoples—Canada—Biography.
Classification: LCC E98.S9 F54 2020 | DDC 362.28089/97071—dc23

Project Director: Dianne Meili
Cover Image: Chloe "Bluebird" Mustooch
Illustrations: Chloe "Bluebird" Mustooch
Cover Design: Gregory Brown

Stony Plain Public Library acknowledges it is in Treaty 6 territory, the traditional territory of the Plains Cree, Woodland Cree, Beaver Cree, Saulteaux, Niisitapi (Blackfoot), Métis, and Nakota Sioux Peoples.

Produced with the assistance of the Government of Alberta.

We acknowledge the financial support of the Government of Canada.
Nous reconnaissons l'appui financier du gouvernement du Canada.

PC: 39-1

FINDING WAKÂ
JAYSEN'S STORY

by Jaysen Flett-Paul

Illustrated by Chloe "Bluebird" Mustooch

ESCHIA BOOKS

Robins are chirping in the poplar trees, and the sunlight turns the water into sparkling diamonds. I gaze up at the cloudless blue sky before I dive into the cold lake. I grab my friend's legs under the water and scare her. We laugh and splash around until we get hungry and ride home on our horses. I joke around and stand up on Daguwa's back to show off, but something in the bush scares him. He kicks his hind legs, and I fall...

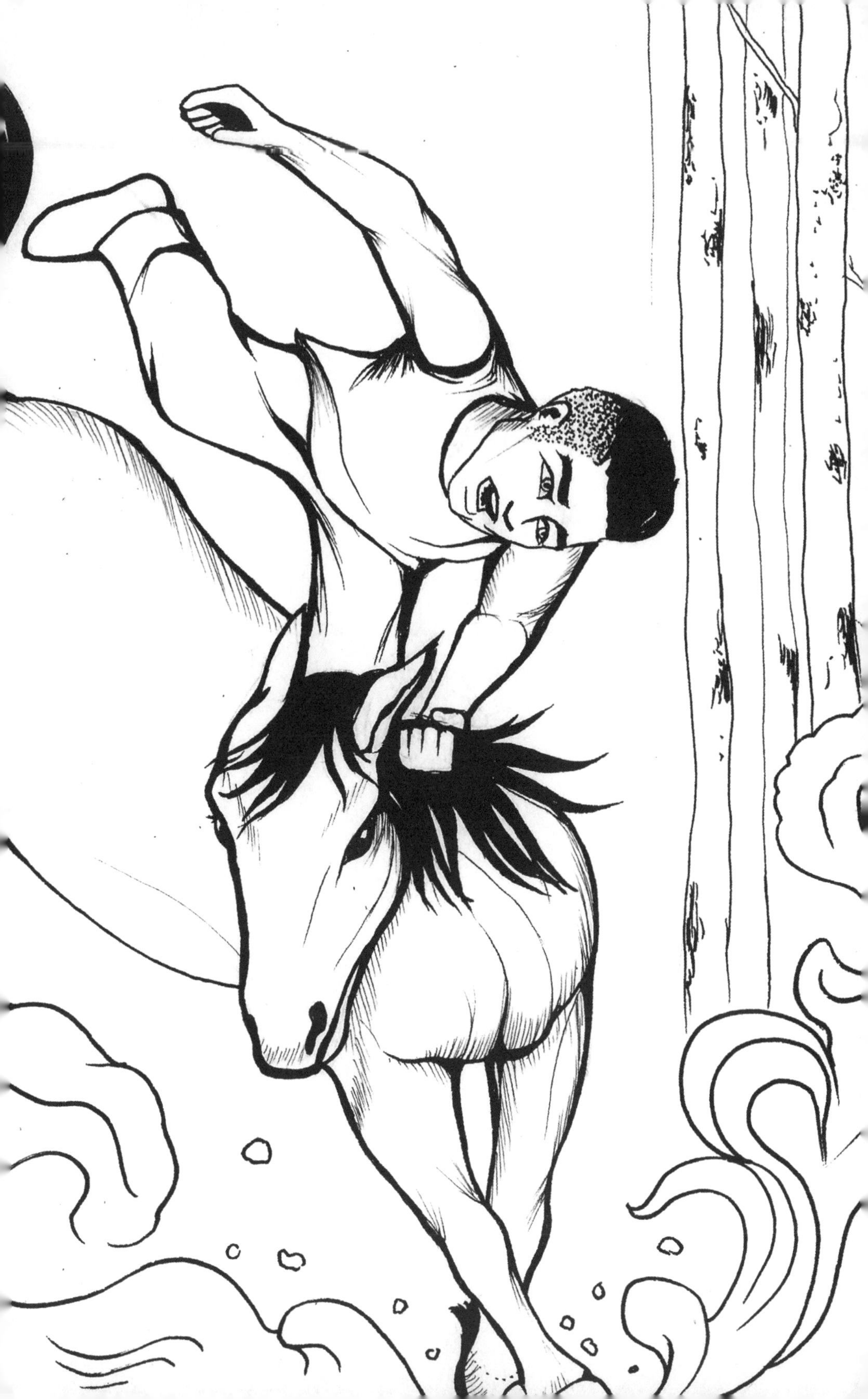

I hit the ground hard and jolt awake.
Blinking, I see my bedroom and slowly
sit up. The hockey posters on the wall,
the clothes on the floor...everything
is normal. I hear a truck revving
somewhere outside, and I flop back
against the pillow. I was only dreaming
about diving into sunlit water and
riding a horse named Daguwa. My
grandmother calls me for breakfast,
and I wonder where my mom is.

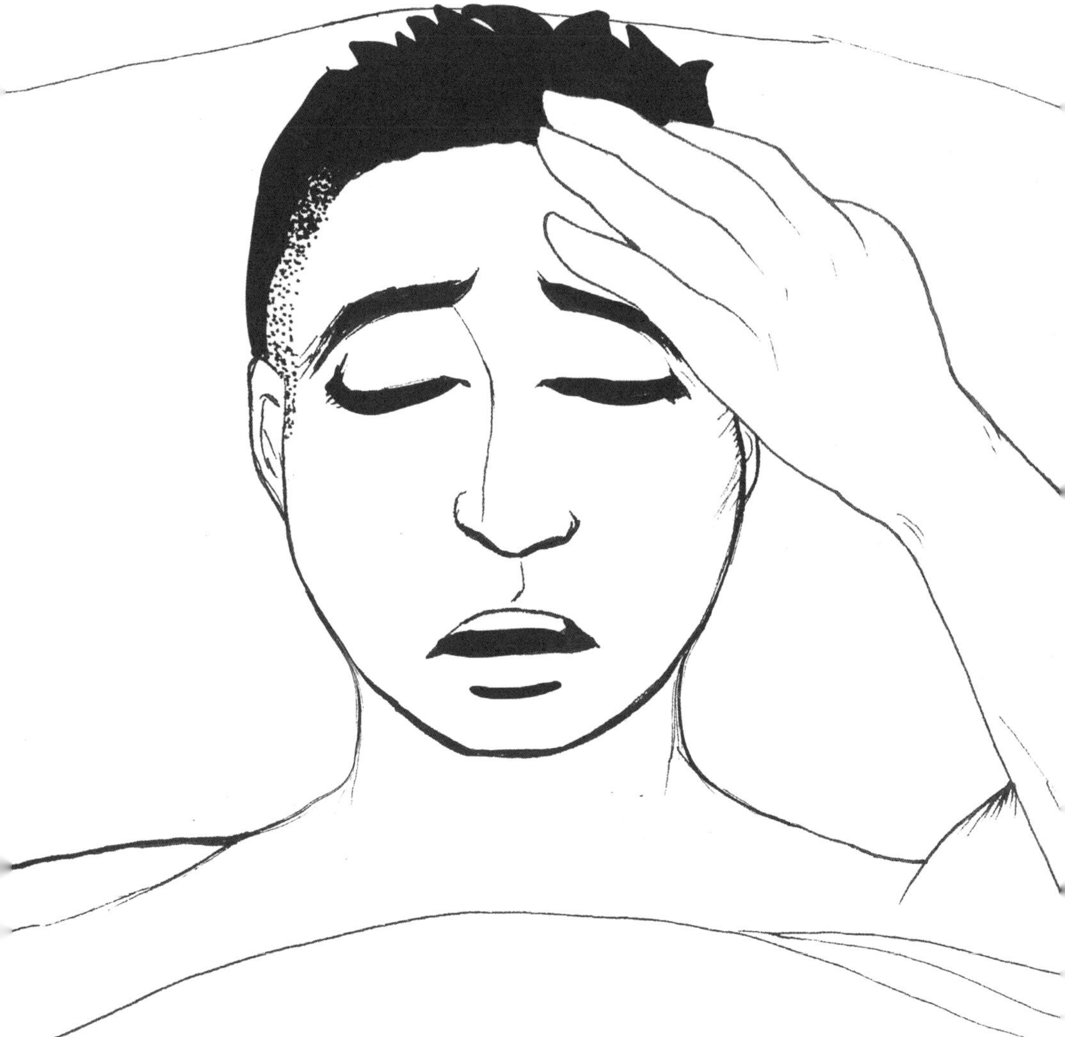

The memories flood back.

It's February, and I'm at a youth pilgrimage. Everyone is gathered for the final celebration. I look into the crowd, expecting to see my mom sitting in the audience, but she's not there. A sick feeling comes over me because I know she wouldn't miss this. Then I see my auntie, and she's crying.

"Let's go see grandma," she says through her tears. No one will tell me what's wrong, but I know it's bad.

Finally, when we get to the car, my uncle tells me, "She's gone." I know my mother is no longer on this earth.

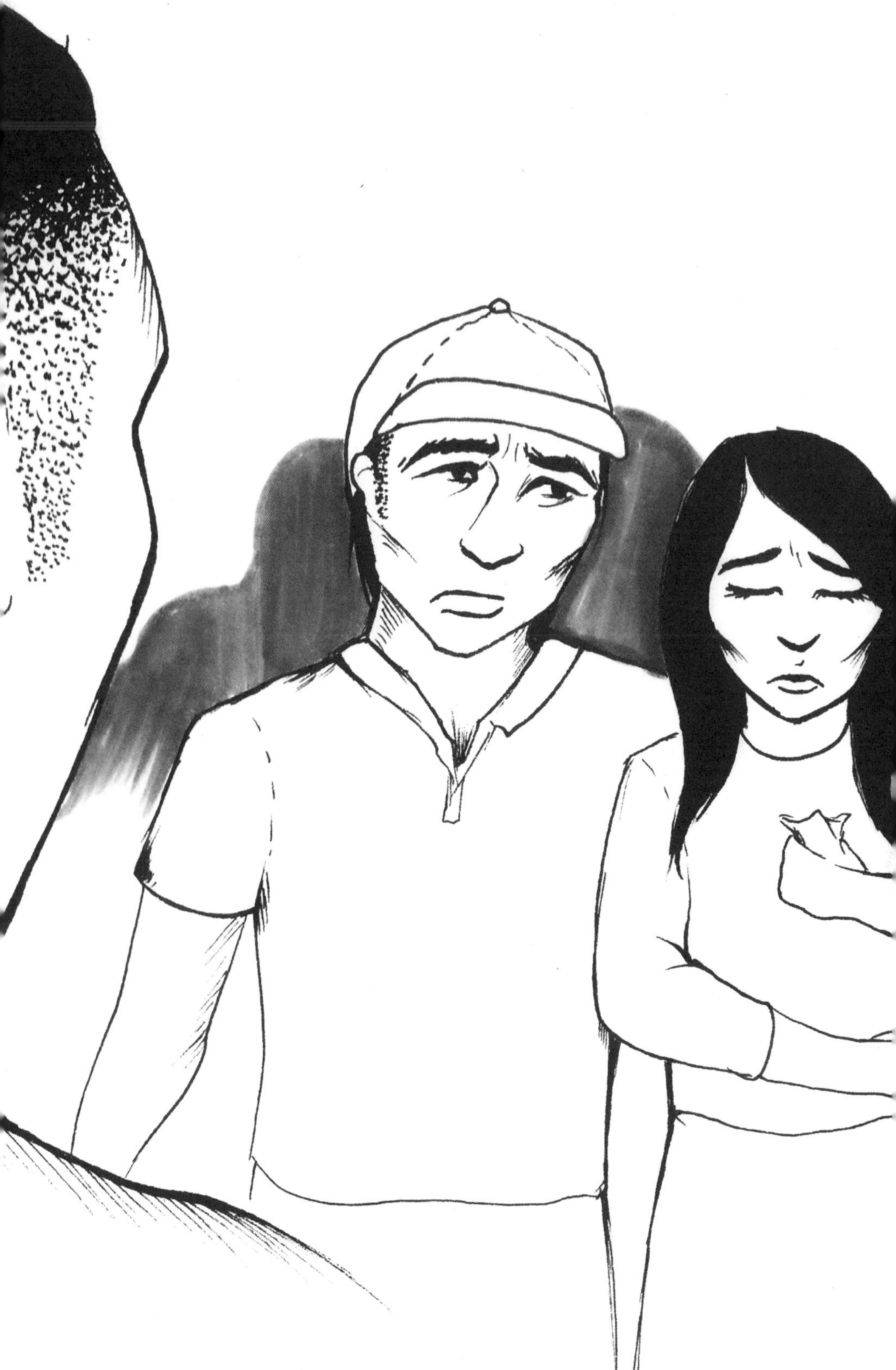

I didn't think I was going to make it during those next few days. Sad is not a word to describe how I felt. I was so close to my mom, but we had a big argument just before she dropped me off at the youth pilgrimage. That was the last time I saw her. I felt so ashamed about the way I acted and what I said. If only I had known I'd never see her again.

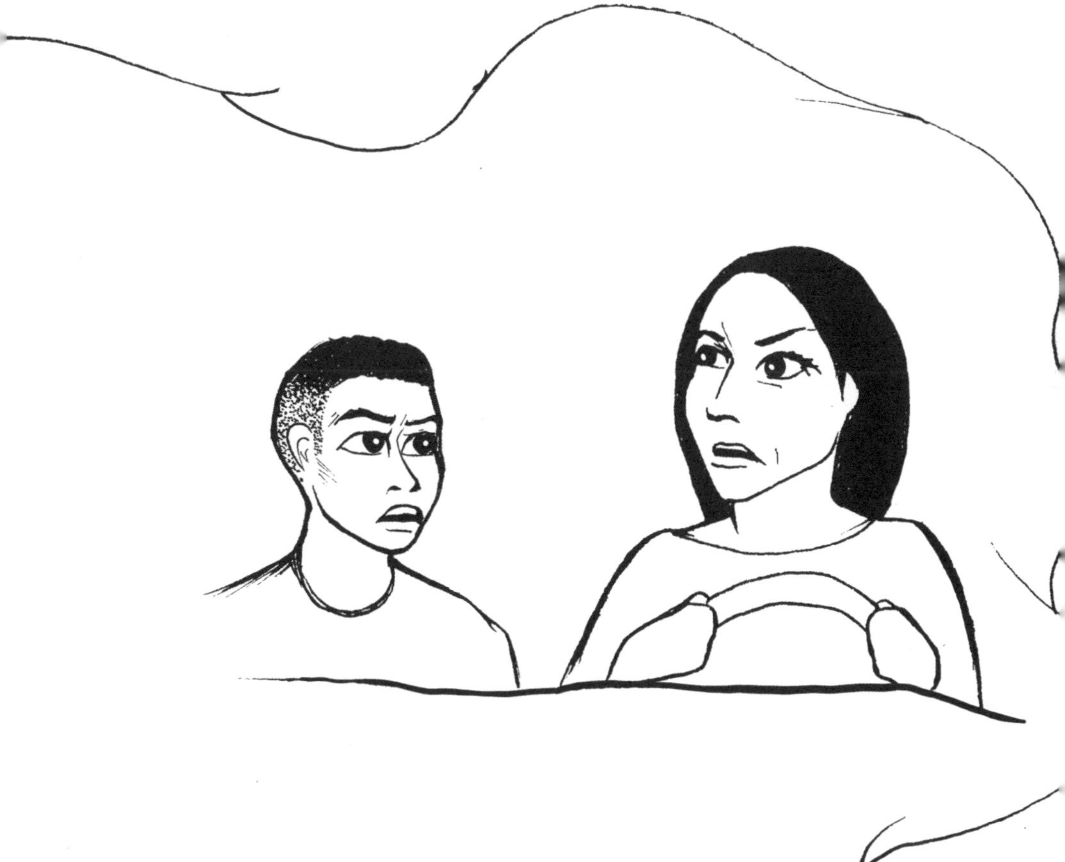

Guilt is an awful feeling. I feel frustrated that I can't turn back time and act differently, that I can't fix everything for my mother and me. I want her to still be here. I want to go places with her and even listen to her advice. Even though we argued, she was usually right about things. I know she loved me.

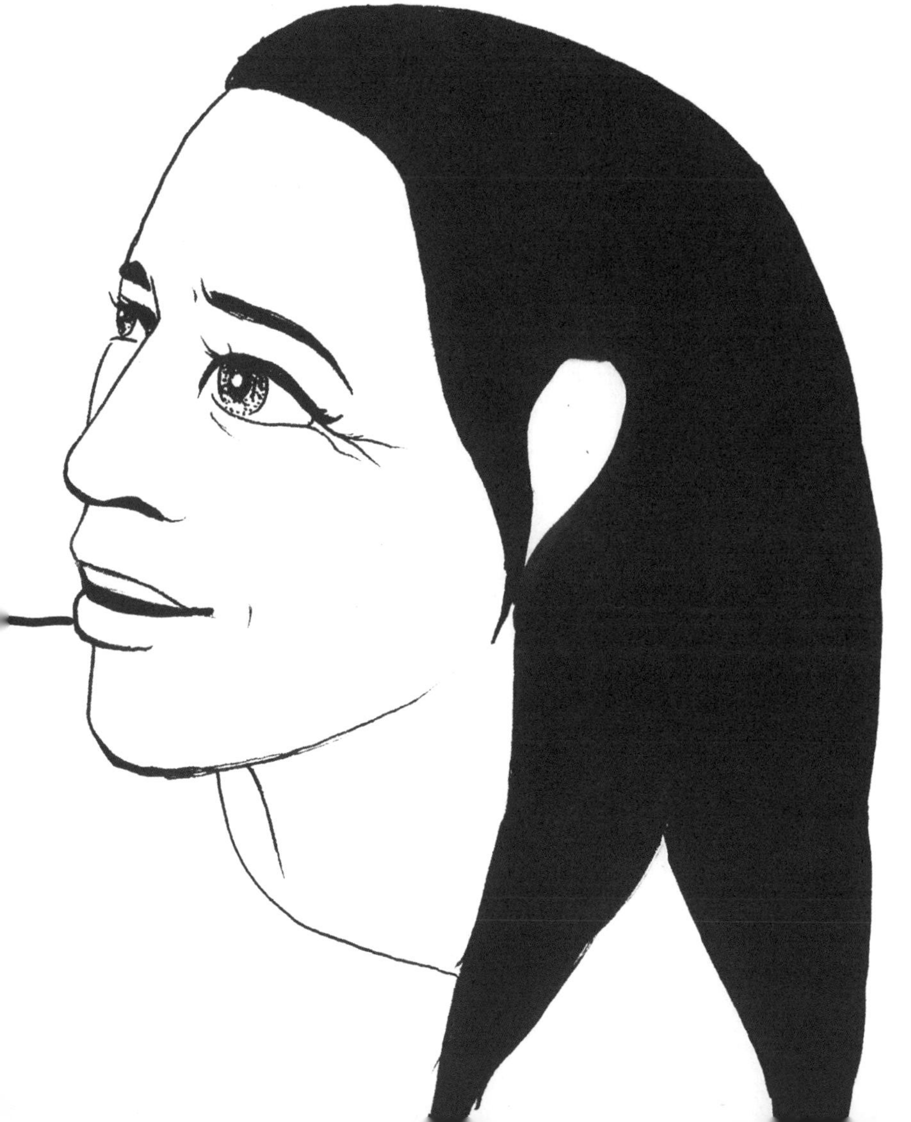

The worst of it all is that I somehow feel responsible for my mother's murder, even though it was someone else who pulled the trigger of the gun that killed her. I wonder if I had been better to her, or if I hadn't gone to the youth pilgrimage, would she be safe and happy today? These questions run through my mind.

It's stressful, and I even think about committing suicide. Lots. But I realize that ending my life will only stop my own pain, and that it will add to the sadness and heartache of my family and friends. I decide to stay on this earth because so many people love me.

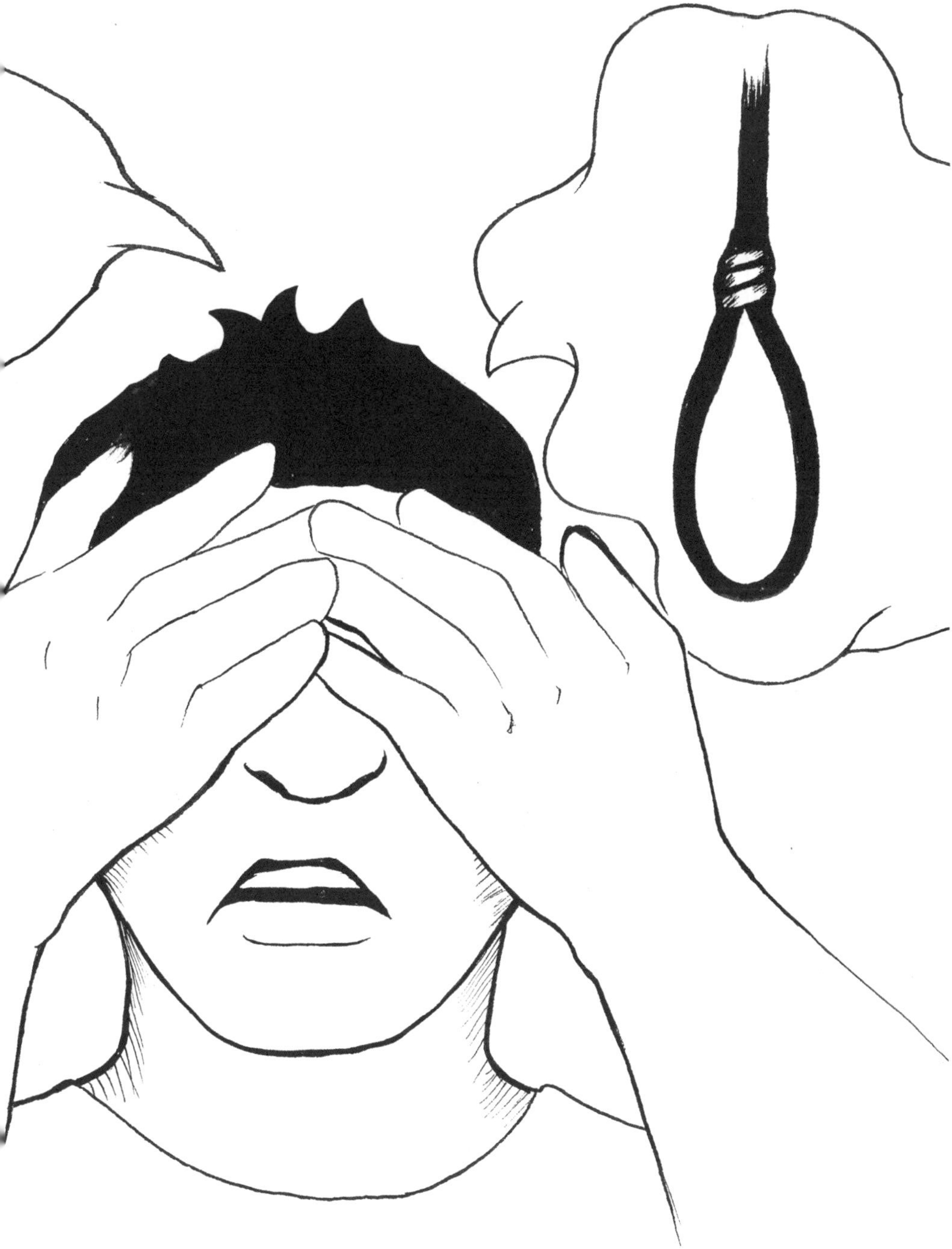

In the deep cold of March, I talk with my Grandfather Willard about my grief. After we sit together for a long time, and I listen to him, I feel better. Even though I lived in the city for eight years, I've always had a connection with him here in my community. He is an open-minded person and very kind. I trust him when he tells me ceremony will help me with my sadness.

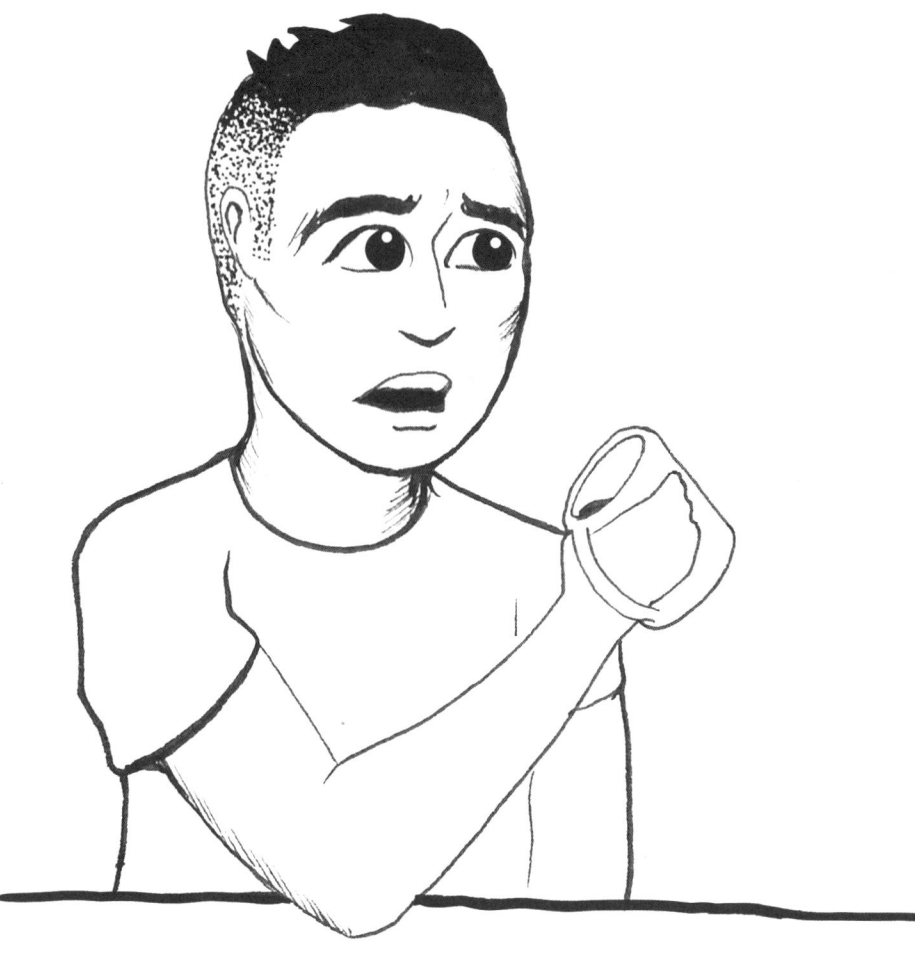

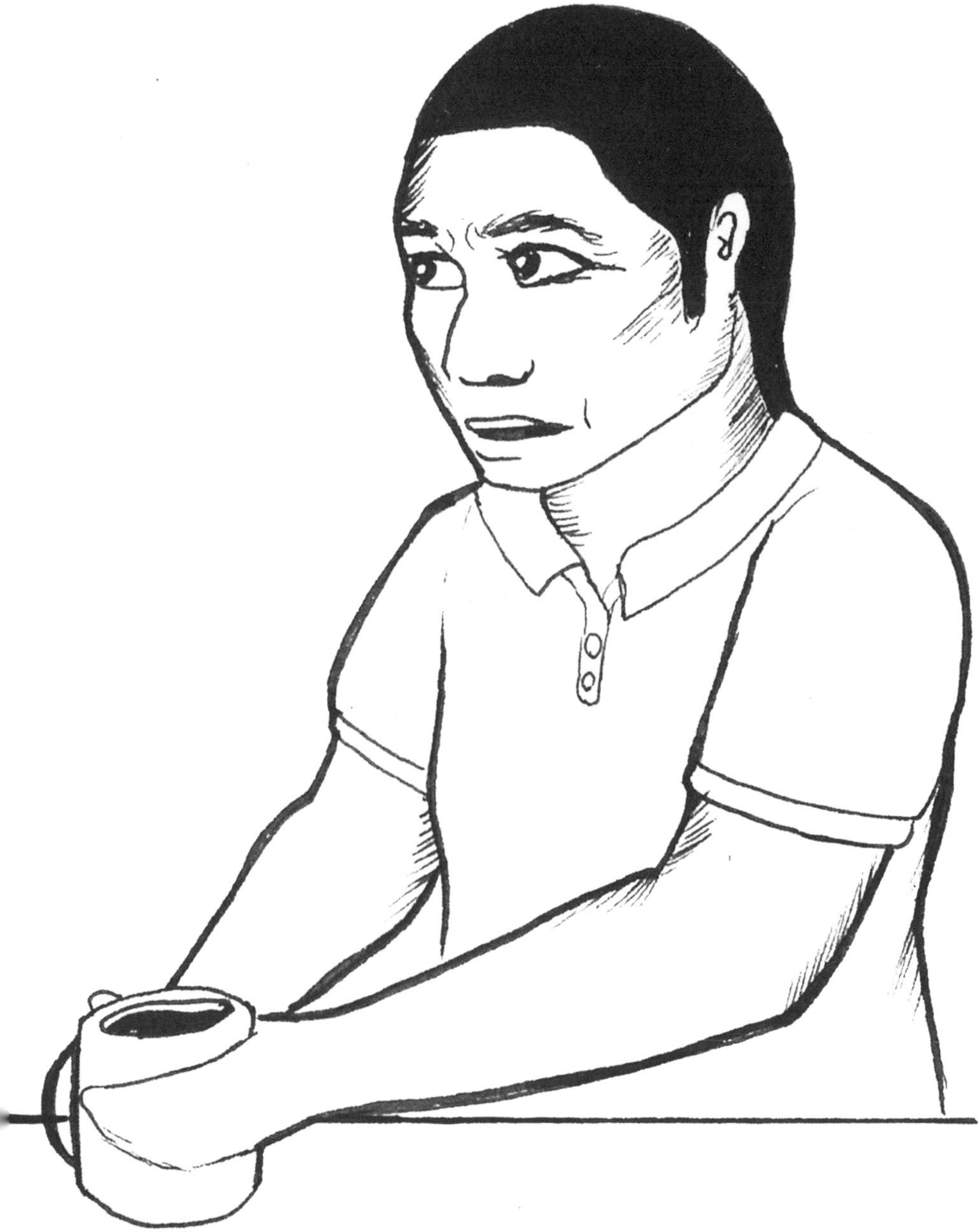

"There is a way of life that will help us," he tells me. "And that is ceremony. We do ceremonies to help us with hardship in life. We need help to overcome our grievances, or when we are sick.

"When you pray in ceremony, something happens, and you realize the Creator is so powerful. Something may happen that lets you know that the Creator, and all of life as you know it, is helping you," my grandfather says.

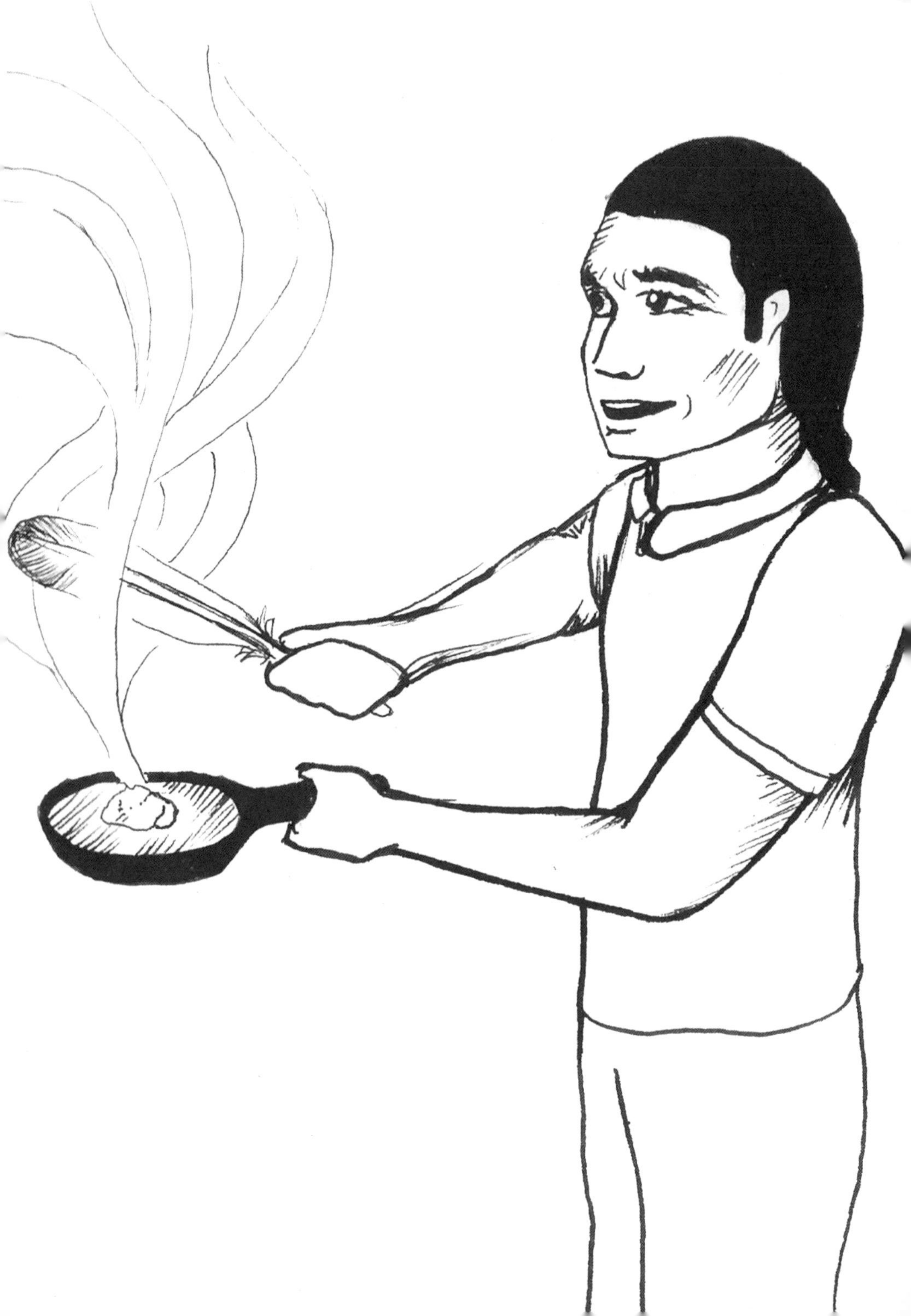

After hearing my grandfather's words, I don't say anything, and so he tells me about something he experienced during a Sundance. One year he was really suffering. He was tired and weak from dancing from dawn to sundown without water or food. He was praying to the Creator to help him make it to the end of the ceremony. The day was really hot with no wind, but out of nowhere came a fresh breeze. The breeze not only cooled him, but revived him and gave him new strength. He understood the Creator was looking after him by sending the wind, and he was able to make it to the end of the ceremony.

"Ceremonial experiences like that make you become more aware of the natural elements and the power of Creation," my grandfather said.

"When we say *Wakâ* in our language, it means the "Great Mystery" who created everything. We can't explain how it works because it's not for our human minds to know."

He asks me to come and sit with him in the *Inimi*, the sweatlodge. I trust him, and so I go with him.

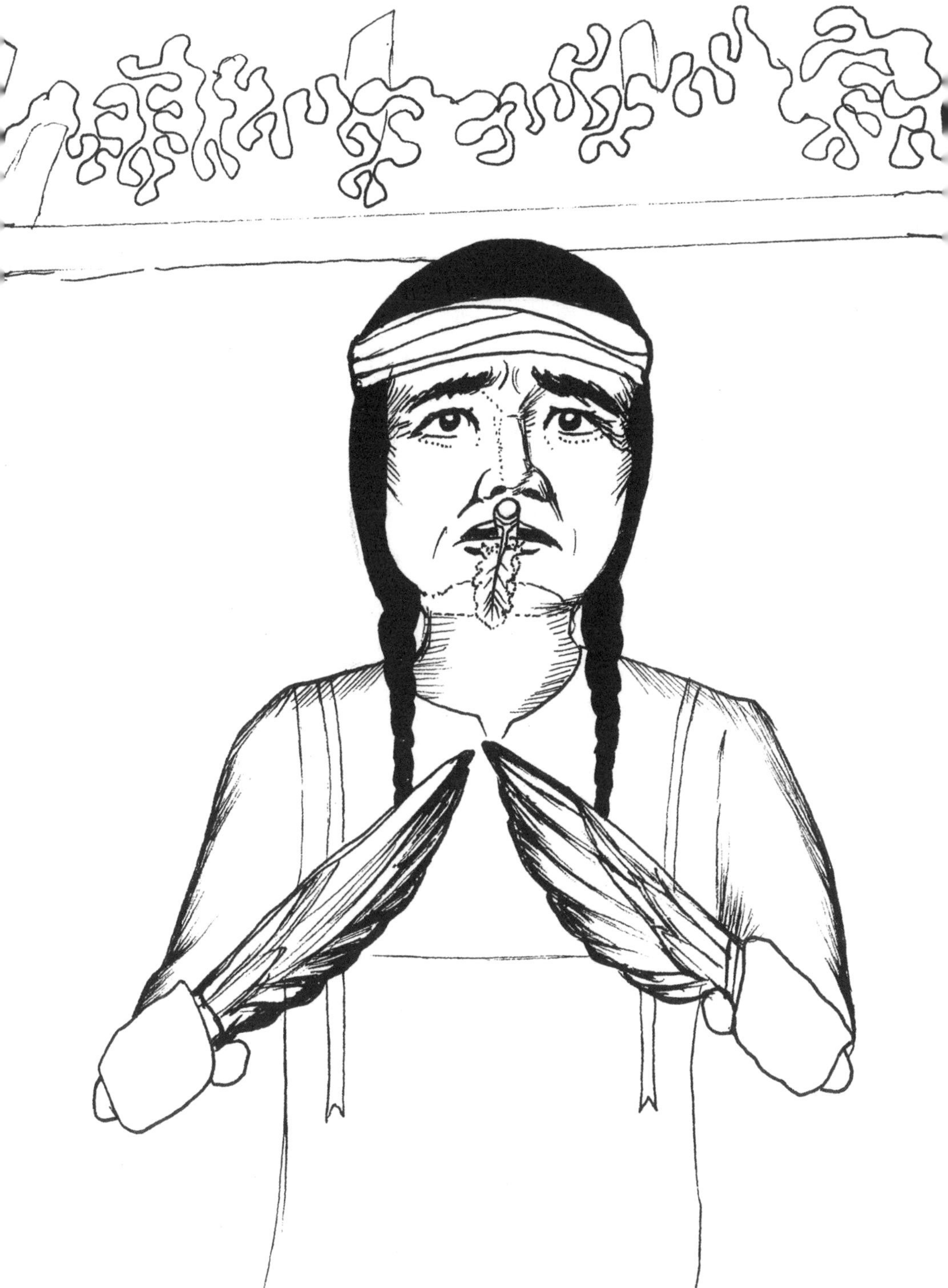

Cade uhiye Wakâ gina.

In the sweat lodge we pray to the Creator, humbling ourselves and asking for help. As the door closes, and the hot rocks glow orange in the darkness, my grandfather splashes water on them. The sacred songs begin, and everyone sitting inside prays for me. They pray for my late mother. Everyone cares about me and how sad I've been feeling. I have never felt like that before. My tears blend with the sweat running down my face. The steam washes over me, and it seems to smooth some of the dark, jagged places in my mind. Some of my sad thoughts are wiped away.

When the *Inimi* is over, I actually feel better. My grandfather tells me I am going to be part of another ceremony this summer. He says I will dance for one day in my Grandfather Charlie's Sundance.

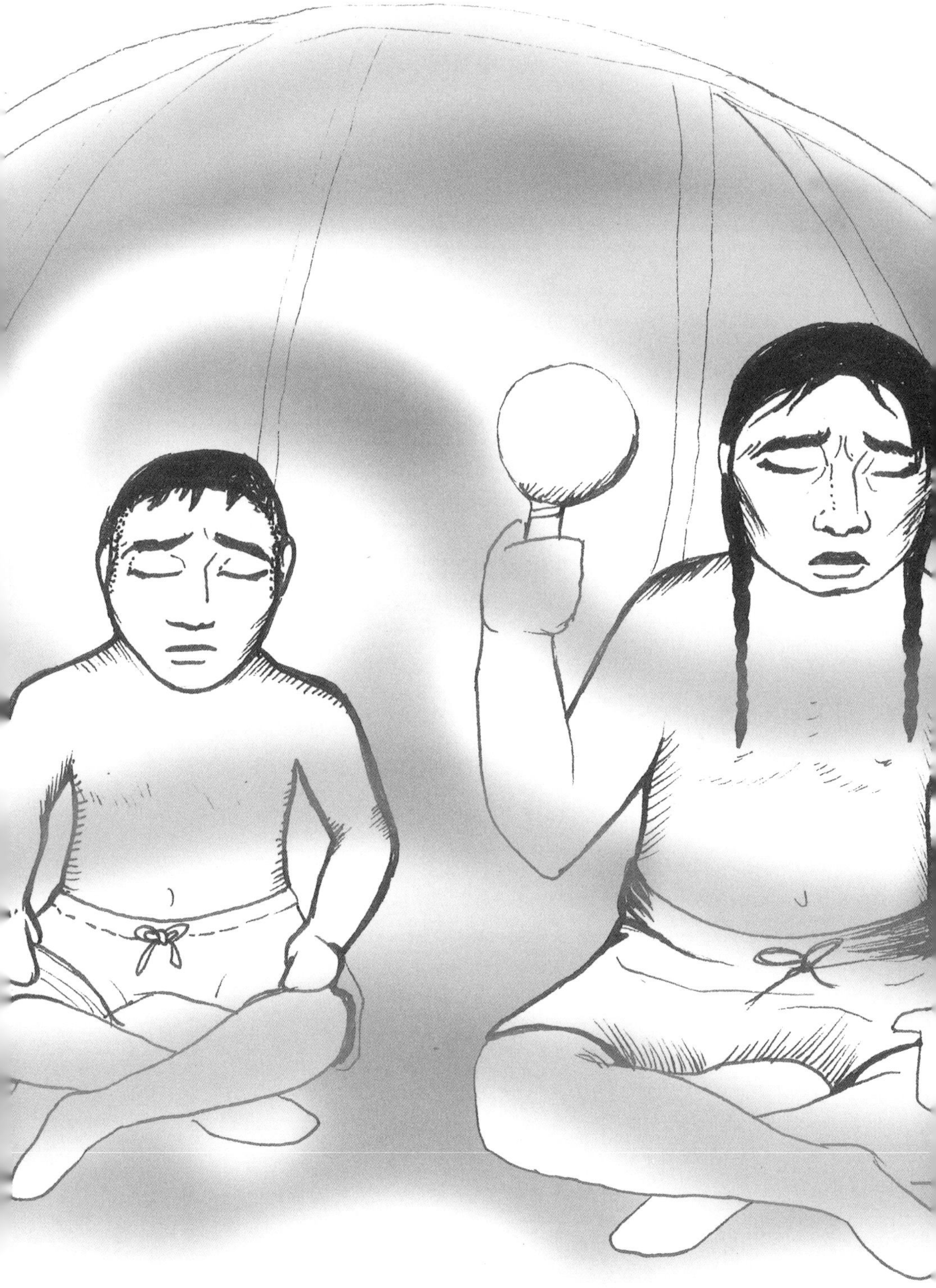

The first winter without my mom is long. The snowy, grey weather hangs on and on, and I feel lost. At least I have my friends. We play pool at the youth centre, and we hit the ice. Our hockey team almost makes it to the provincials. I score two goals in our last game. It is my grandma's birthday, and I tell her that is her present.

But through it all, I miss my mom. Every day I wish I could tell her stuff and ask her questions. She wasn't perfect, but I loved her, and she was always close by.

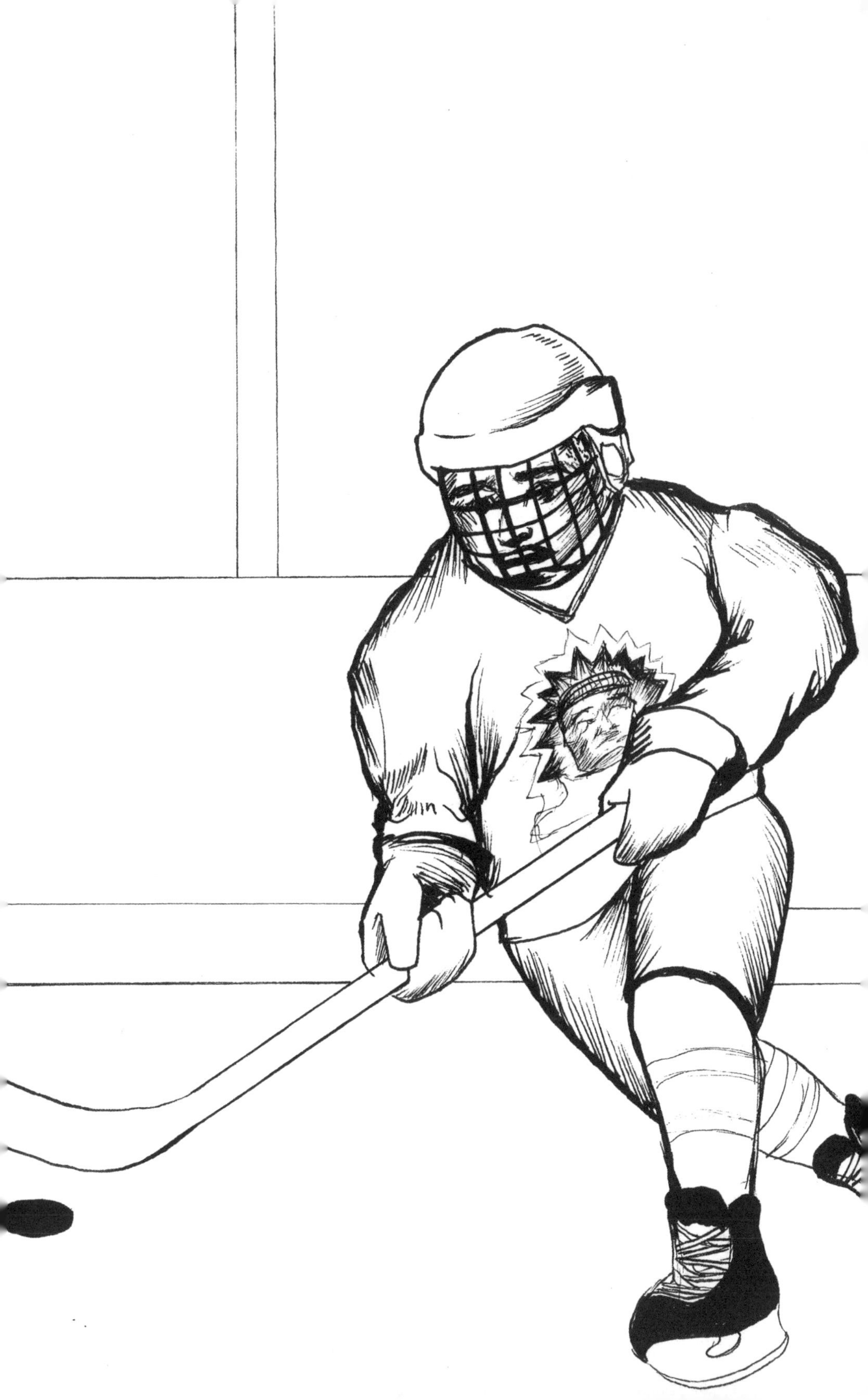

The snow finally melts by May long weekend, and I'm glad I made it through winter. Still, I pretty much keep to myself. People think it's because I'm sad all the time. Really, it's because I want to stay away from negativity. I have a couple of good "brudders," and we are already talking about camping out at Birch Lake this summer. It's good to have something to look forward to.

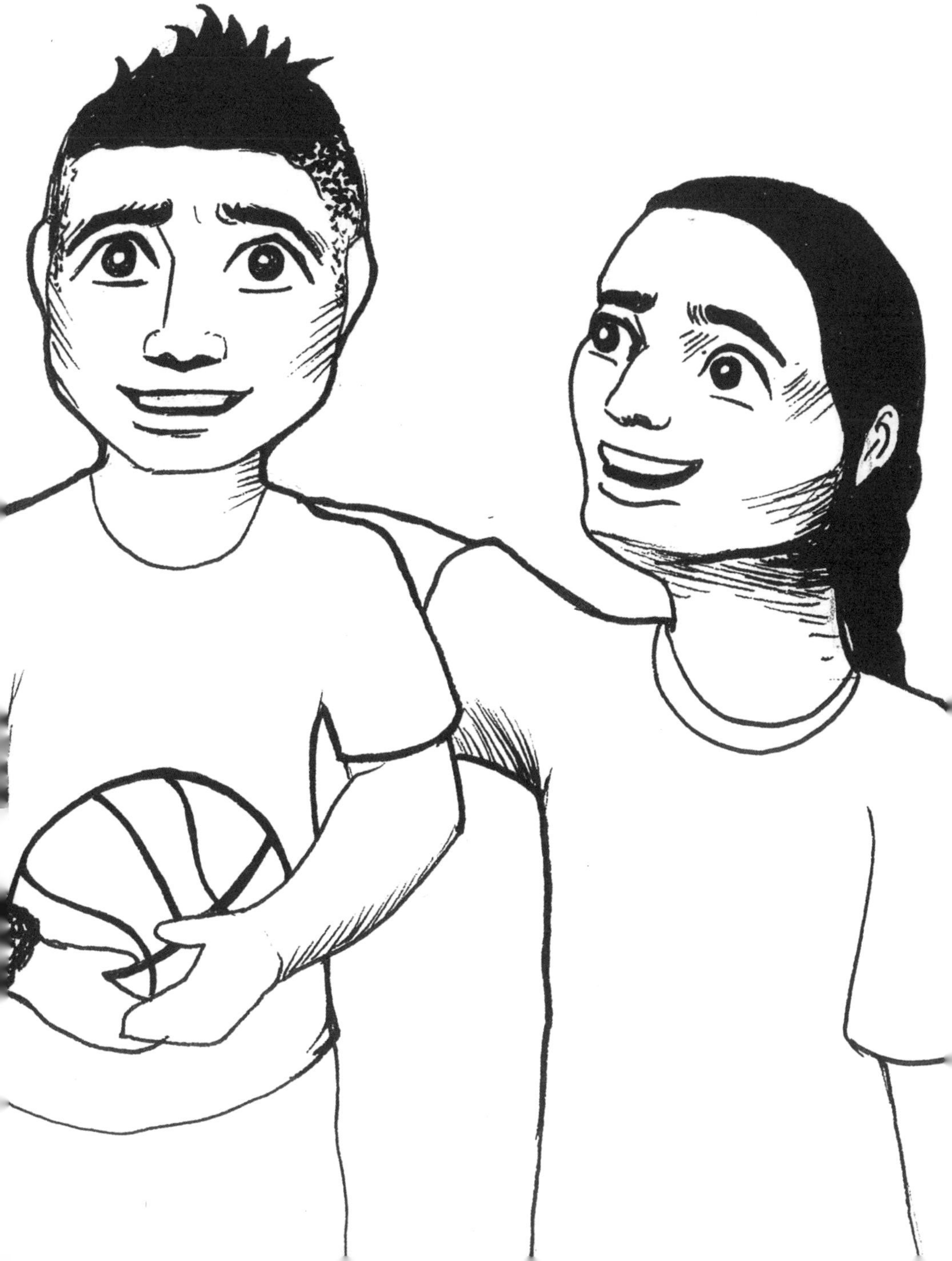

Before I know it, it's July and day one of the Sundance.

The sun is just coming up, and the robins are singing. They remind me of the dream I had about summer days after my mother died. I was swimming in the lake and riding on the back of a horse named Daguwa. Was that only six months ago? It seems like years.

I work hard with some other youth, hauling wood and rocks for the *Inimi* that is held before the Sundance begins. My grandfather says I should feel happy with myself for helping to get ready for it. I'm not only helping myself, I'm also helping the other people who will come and dance.

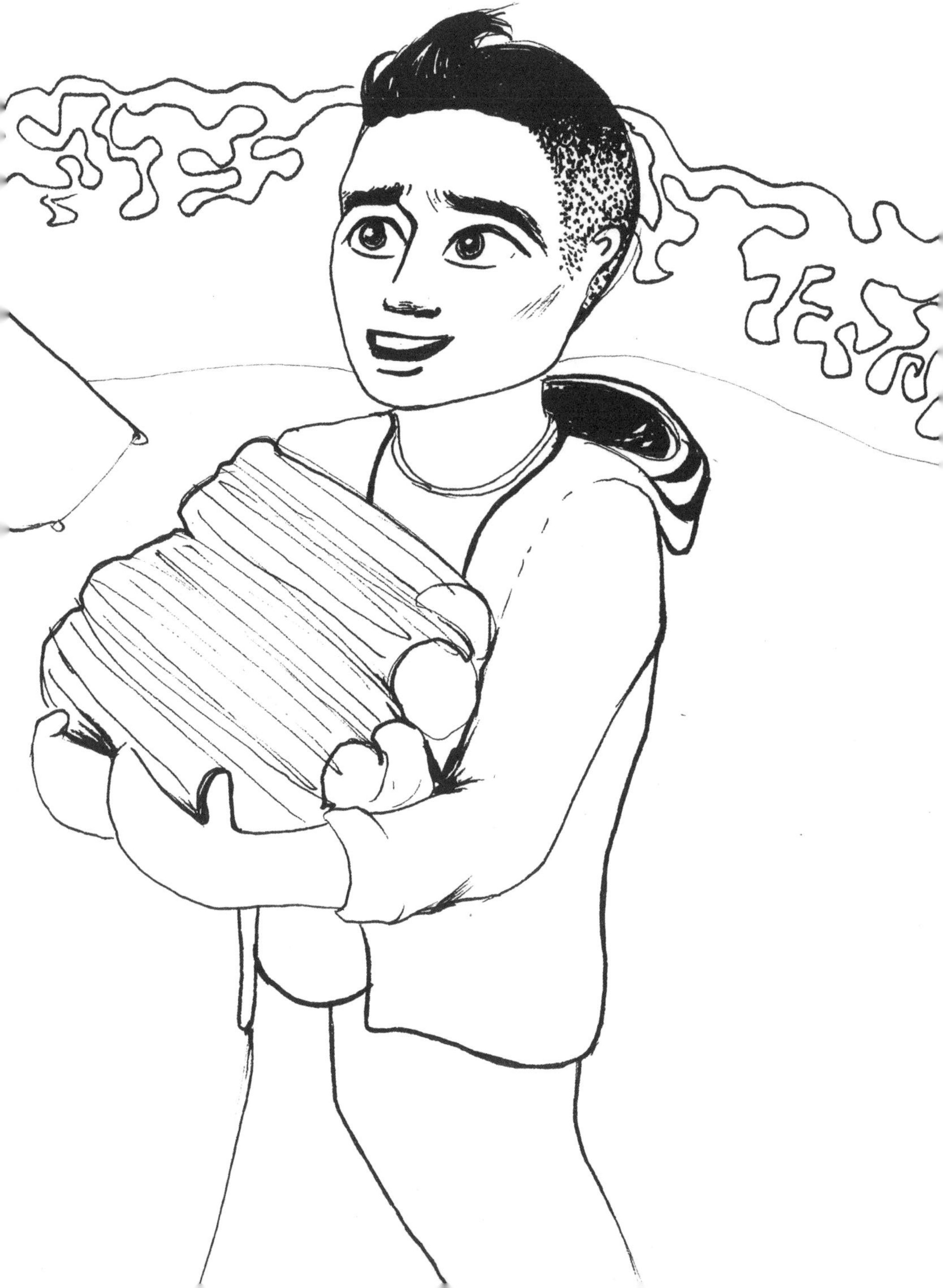

I dance beside my grandfather. I dance for my mother and my grandmother, and my brothers and sisters. I never get hungry, but I do get thirsty. I now understand something that my grandfather told me about what happens when a person goes without food or water for spiritual purposes. You experience your thirst and hunger, and you may want to quit, but you have patience. And by passing through those tests of the body, you move beyond, facing your earthly fears to become Spirit. Then everything changes and other spirits—those of animals and the water, wind, rain and earth—draw close. They take pity on you, and they come to help you. I feel the spirit of my mother near me.

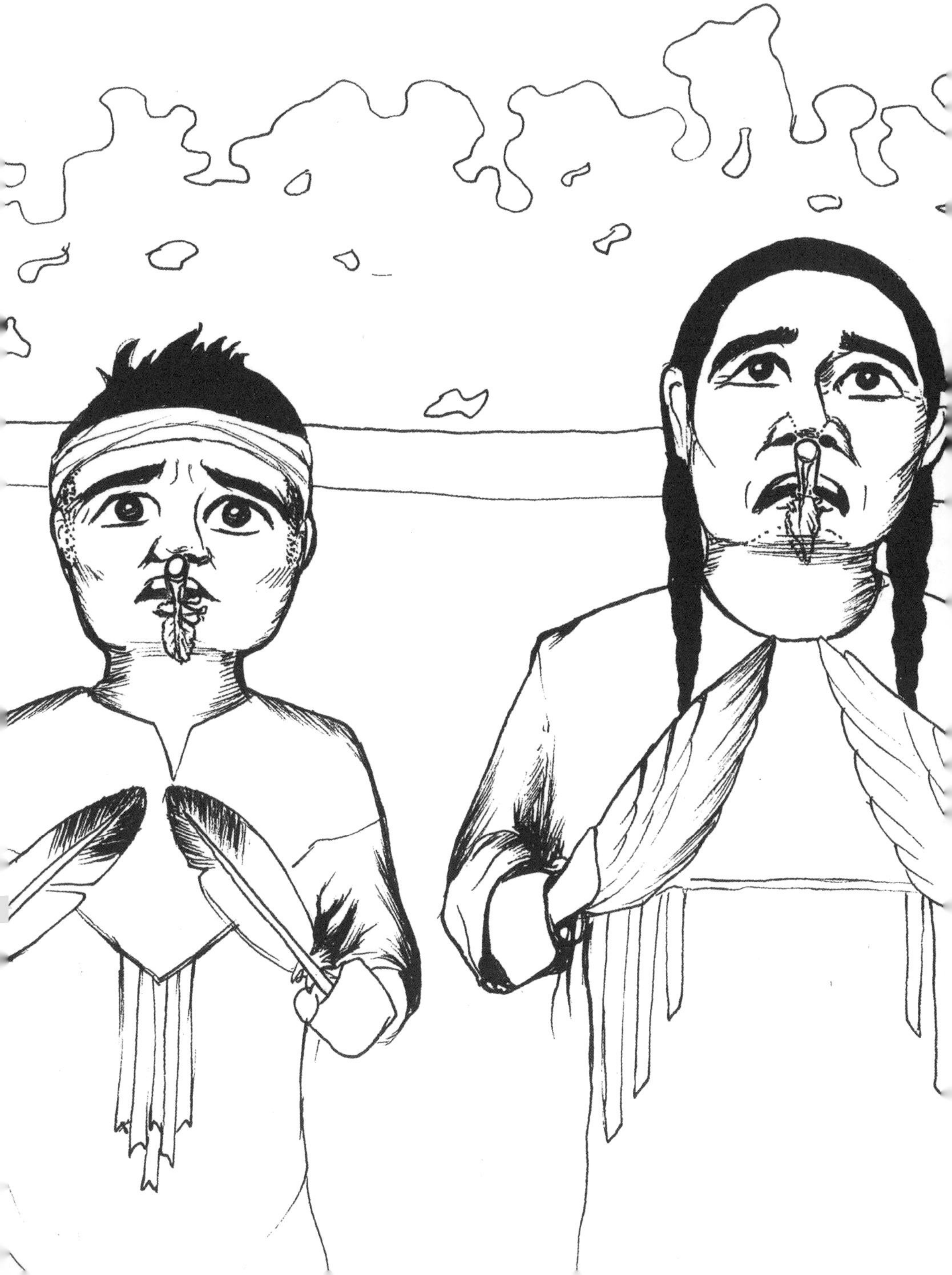

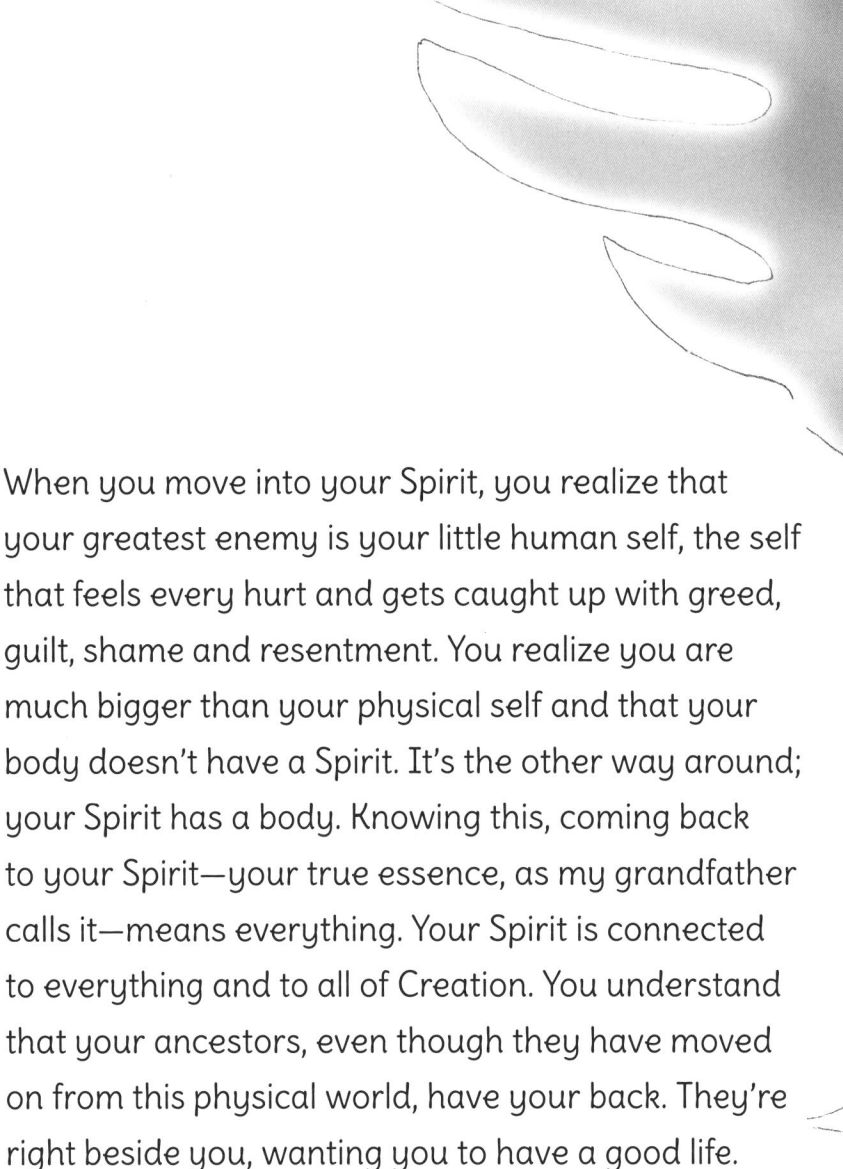

When you move into your Spirit, you realize that your greatest enemy is your little human self, the self that feels every hurt and gets caught up with greed, guilt, shame and resentment. You realize you are much bigger than your physical self and that your body doesn't have a Spirit. It's the other way around; your Spirit has a body. Knowing this, coming back to your Spirit—your true essence, as my grandfather calls it—means everything. Your Spirit is connected to everything and to all of Creation. You understand that your ancestors, even though they have moved on from this physical world, have your back. They're right beside you, wanting you to have a good life.

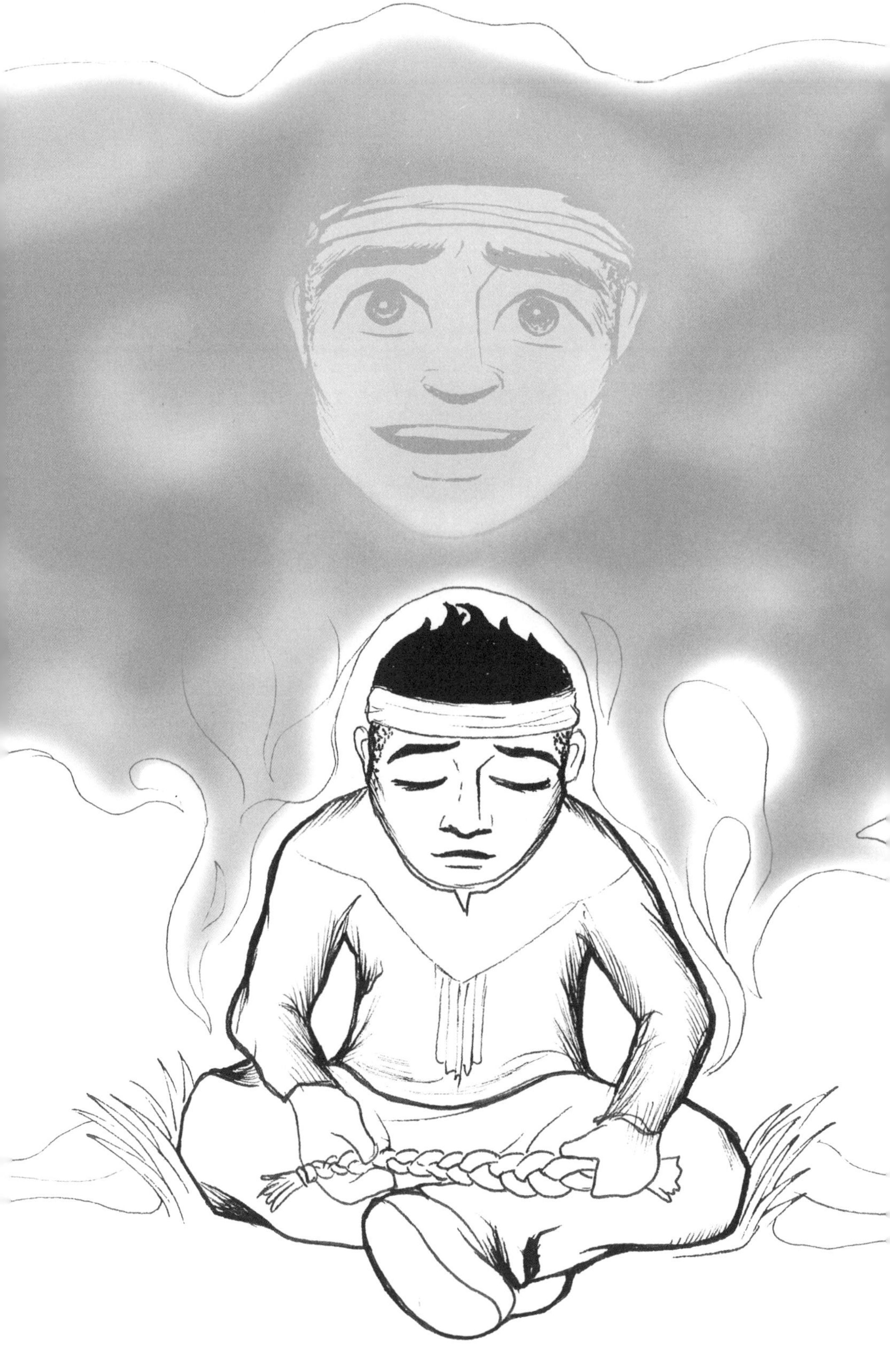

The Sundance stays with me. I will never forget the sound of the eagle bone whistles and the Sundance songs. It was good to dance with my community in a circle. As fall comes around again and school starts, I feel stronger, like I am getting to know who I really am.

Through ceremony and what my grandfather tells me, I realize my mom is with me. She never left. Spirit does not die. I know she knows I'm sorry about arguing with her. I don't carry all that guilt anymore.

I won't lie. Some days I feel as lost as ever, but the ceremonies are helping me. They connect me to my Spirit. And the Sundance is pretty special. People wait all year for it. I will dance two days next summer.

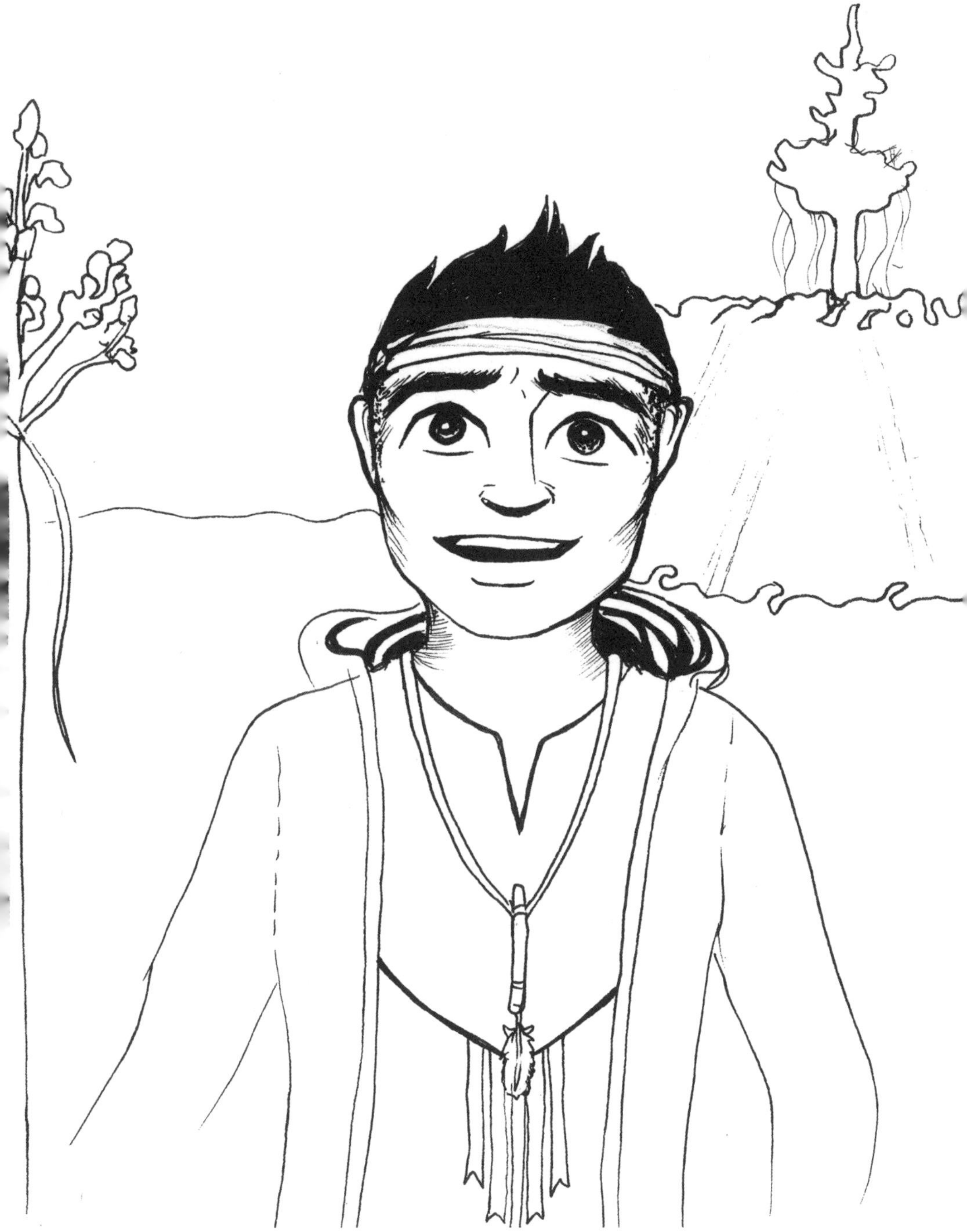

If you are struggling with stuff and your life feels like one big mistake, try talking to an Elder in your community. They can guide you through ceremony and back to Yourself, your Spirit. You are a worthwhile person. You just have to believe that.

This is me, Jaysen Flett-Paul of Alexis Nakota Sioux Nation, telling you that the Creator is always with you, and if you trust in *Wakâ,* you will be helped.